MW01223086

Language Launch

Volume 1

UNIT 1 | Welcome to School

Printed in the U.S.A.

ISBN 978-0-358-86408-0

r12.23

3 4 5 6 7 8 9 10 0607 32 31 30 29 28 27 26 25 24

4500885123

Table of Contents

Unit 1: Welcome to School

 ## Make Observations

Look at the image. Discuss what you see.

Draw or take notes to help you.

Meet Elodie!

**Elodie is your host for Unit 1: Welcome to School.
She will guide you through the unit by giving you
helpful information!**

**What grade
are you in?**

I'm in the 9th grade,
and I love my new school!

**What is your
favorite subject?**

I like English class the most!
I love writing poems.

**What is your
favorite activity?**

My favorite activity is playing
soccer with my friends.

**What are all of
your languages?**

I speak and write in both
Haitian-Creole and English.
I can speak French too!

View the Anchor Video

Welcome to school! At school, students learn. Students also make friends. Let's watch a video to learn more about school.

Vocabulary Builder

1. Say It   **2.** See It   **3.** Read It   **4.** Write It

school

school
(noun)

School is a place where you can learn.

Word _____
   school
Translation _____

Make Connections _____

_____

students

stu • dents
(noun)

Students learn at school.

Word _____
   students
Translation _____

Make Connections _____

_____

teacher

teach • er
(noun)

Students learn from a **teacher**.

Word _____
    teacher

Translation _____

Make Connections _____

_____

friends

friends
(noun)

Students meet **friends** at school.

Word _____
    friends

Translation _____

Make Connections _____

_____

Vocabulary Review

school

teacher

students

friends

Share translations with a partner.

**LANGUAGE TO
SHARE TRANSLATIONS**

What language do you speak?

I speak (language).

·····································

Can you share a word in (language)?

The (language) word for _____ is _____.

Write the best word under each image.

_____

_____

_____

_____

| friends | school | students | teacher |

View and Respond

Watch the video again.

1. Choose the sentence that matches the picture.

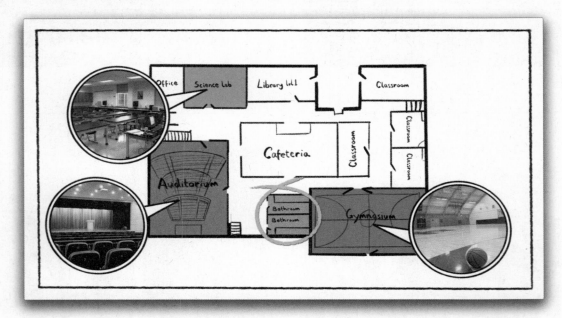

☐ There are many places at **school**.

☐ There are many **students** at school.

2. Choose the sentence that matches the picture.

☐ This is Elodie's **teacher**, Mr. Patel.

☐ This is Elodie's **friend**, Andrew.

3. Choose the sentence that matches the picture.

☐ Elodie was a new **student** last year.

☐ Elodie made new **friends** at school.

View the Anchor Video

Watch the video again.

 ## Vocabulary Builder

1. Say It   **2.** See It   **3.** Read It   **4.** Write It

---

read

read
(verb)

Students **read** books.

Word _____
     read

Translation _____

Make Connections _____

_____

---

write

write
(verb)

Students **write** sentences.

Word _____
     write

Translation _____

Make Connections _____

_____

listen

lis • ten
(verb)

Students **listen** to the teacher.

Word _____
    listen

Translation _____

Make Connections _____

_____

speak

speak
(verb)

Students **speak** with their friends.

Word _____
    speak

Translation _____

Make Connections _____

_____

 Vocabulary Review

read   listen

write   speak

Share translations with a partner.

LANGUAGE TO
SHARE TRANSLATIONS

What language do you speak?
I speak (<u>language</u>).

• •

Can you share a word in (<u>language</u>)?
The (<u>language</u>) word for _____ is _____.

Writing

✎ View and Take Notes

Watch the video again. Take notes.

1. Elodie was a new _____ last year.

   Now, she can show you around her _____.

2. First stop is English class. Her _____

   suggested she join the poetry club.

3. Next stop is the cafeteria. Elodie asks her _____

   Andrew for help.

4. Last stop is the soccer field! Elodie loves being on the team.

WORD BANK			🧩
Vocabulary			
school	student	teacher	friend

Make Connections

Underline the things you want to do at school.

At school, I want to ...

- speak in class

- read new books

- meet new friends

- learn from my teacher

Partner A, ask questions. Partner B, respond. Then switch roles.

A: What do you want to do at school?

B: I want to _____

   at school.

A: What else do you want to do at school?

B: I also want to _____

   at school.

Meet and Greet

Hello! My name is Elodie. How are you? At school, we meet people and make friends. Let's learn how to introduce ourselves when we meet a person for the first time.

 Vocabulary Builder

1. Say It   **2.** See It   **3.** Read It   **4.** Write It

hello
hel • lo
(greeting)

Hello! How are you?

Word _____
       hello

Translation _____

Make Connections _____

_____

name
name
(noun)

What is your **name**? My **name** is Alana.

Word _____
      name

Translation _____

Make Connections _____

_____

introduce

in • tro • **duce**
(verb)

When I **introduce** myself, I say my name.

Word _____
introduce

Translation _____

Make Connections _____

_____

meet

meet
(verb)

It's nice to **meet** you.

Word _____
meet

Translation _____

Make Connections _____

_____

ask

ask
(verb)

I **ask** questions when I don't understand.

Word _____
ask

Translation _____

Make Connections _____

_____

thank you
thank you
(exclamation)

I'm fine. **Thank you** for asking.

Word _____
      thank you

Translation _____

Make Connections _____

_____

goodbye
good • bye
(exclamation)

Goodbye! Have a nice day.

Word _____
      goodbye

Translation _____

Make Connections _____

_____

Vocabulary Review

hello   introduce   ask   goodbye

name   meet   thank you

Share translations with a partner.

LANGUAGE TO SHARE TRANSLATIONS

What language do you speak?

I speak (language).

••

Can you share a word in (language)?

The (language) word for _____ is _____.

Language Builder

How to Introduce Yourself

- Say, "Hello" or "Hi" to a new person.

- Tell them your name: "My name is _____."

- Ask, "What is your name?" or "What's your name?"

- Say, "It's nice to meet you. How are you?"

- Say, "I'm fine, thank you. How are you?"

   I'm great.   I'm fine.   I don't feel great.

Practice greetings.

Hello.

Good morning.

Good afternoon.

Good evening.

Good night.

Practice introducing yourself.

My name is _____. It's nice to meet you.

Match the question or phrase to the response.

What's your name? ◯	◯ I'm fine, thank you.
It's nice to meet you. ◯	◯ Bye! Have a nice day.
How are you? ◯	◯ My name is Juan.
Goodbye! ◯	◯ It's nice to meet you too.

Listen Up

Listen to the conversation.

 Hello! My name is Mateo. What's your name?

 Hi! My name is Serene. It's nice to meet you.

It's nice to meet you too. How are you?

I'm fine, thank you. How are you?

I'm doing well, thanks. Goodbye, Serene!

Goodbye, Mateo!

Talk About It

Partner A, **introduce yourself.** Partner B, **respond. Then switch roles.**

A: Hello! My name is _____.
   (Name)

   What's your name?

B: Hi! My name is _____.
   (Name)

   It's nice to meet you.

A: It's nice to meet you too. How are you?

B: I'm fine, thank you. How are you?

A: I'm doing well, thanks. Goodbye,

   _____!
   (Name)

B: Goodbye, _____!
   (Name)

Make Observations

Look at the pictures. Discuss what you see. Take notes to help you.

1. _____

_____

_____

_____

2. _____

_____

_____

_____

3. _____

_____

_____

_____

4. _____

_____

_____

_____

5. _____

_____

_____

_____

WORD BANK

Greetings

bowing	making eye contact	shaking hands
hugging	saying "Hello"	waving

LANGUAGE TO OBSERVE

What do you see?

I see people ____.

What else do you see?

I also see ____.

Read and Respond

Read the text. Then complete the sentences.

United States

Japan

France

New Zealand

China

1   How do you **introduce** yourself? In the United States, it is important to make eye contact. People say, "It's nice to **meet** you!" the first time they **meet** a new friend. Sometimes they shake hands.

2   There are many ways to say **hello**. In Japan, people bow to greet each other. In France, people may kiss the air or each other's cheeks. In New Zealand, the Māori people have a traditional greeting called a *hongi*. They press their noses together. In China, people greet the oldest person first. How do people you know say **hello**?

1. People bow to greet each other in _____.

   (a) France

   (b) Japan

   (c) New Zealand

2. People press their noses together in _____.

   (a) China

   (b) New Zealand

   (c) the United States

3. In the United States, when people meet a new friend, they _____

   (a) bow to each other.

   (b) say, "It's nice to meet you!"

   (c) kiss each other on the cheek.

Write About It

 Remember!

When you meet a new person, say, "Hi" or "Hello." Tell your new friend your name. Say, "It's nice to meet you." When you leave, say, "Goodbye" or "Bye."

Write about introducing yourself in English.

1. When you meet a new person, say, "Hi" or "_____!"

2. Tell your new friend your _____.

3. Say, "It's nice to _____ you!

4. When you leave, say, "_____" or "Bye."

WORD BANK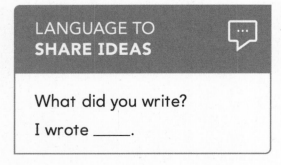

Vocabulary

goodbye   hello   meet   name   thank you

LANGUAGE TO SHARE IDEAS

What did you write?

I wrote ____.

Write a Note

Write a note to your teacher. Introduce yourself.

Dear _____,
       (Teacher's Name)

    My name is _____.
              (Name)

It's nice to _____ you.
       (action)

One thing I want you to know about me is _____
                                         (fact about you)

_____.

One question I want to ask is _____
                             (question)

_____?

_____ for being my teacher.
(Thank you/Thanks)

    Your student,

    _____
     (Name)

> Excellent job! You just learned how to introduce yourself to a new person. Now, tell your partner what you do when you meet a new person: *When I meet a new person, I say (greeting).*

From A to Z

We use letters to read and spell words and to form sentences. Let's learn the letters in the alphabet so that you can read and write in English.

 Learn the Alphabet

Letters of the Alphabet

The English **alphabet** has 26 **letters**. Each letter has an **uppercase**, or **capital**, symbol and a **lowercase** symbol.

Letters **a**, **e**, **i**, **o**, and **u** are **vowels**. The other letters are **consonants**. The letter **y** can be a consonant or a vowel.

Read the alphabet. Point to each letter and say the letter name.

The English Alphabet					
Aa	Bb	Cc	Dd	Ee	Ff
Gg	Hh	Ii	Jj	Kk	Ll
Mm	Nn	Oo	Pp	Qq	Rr
Ss	Tt	Uu	Vv	Ww	Xx
Yy	Zz				

Language Builder

Uppercase and Lowercase Letters

Letters can be **uppercase** or **lowercase**.

uppercase → **A a** ← lowercase

Start names with **an uppercase letter**.

- Names of people: *Mr. Zamora*   *Mitali*
- Names of places: *Los Angeles*
- Names of languages: *English*

Start sentences with **an uppercase letter**.

The English alphabet has 26 letters.

Trace each uppercase and lowercase letter with your finger.

Aa Bb Cc Dd Ee Ff

Gg Hh Ii Jj Kk Ll

Mm Nn Oo Pp Qq Rr

Ss Tt Uu Vv Ww Xx

Yy Zz

Write your name. Start with an uppercase letter.

My name is _____.

Listen Up

Listen to the conversation.

▶ Hi, Chris! How do you spell your name?

Hello, Maria! I spell my name C – h – r – i - s.

Could you please repeat that?

Sure! I spell my name C – h – r – i - s.
The *C* is uppercase.

Talk About It

Partner A, **ask questions.** Partner B, **respond. Then switch roles.**

A: Hi, _____! How do you spell your name?
   (Name)

B: Hello! I spell my name _____.
                          (letters)

A: Could you please repeat that?

B: Sure! I spell my name _____.
                         (letters)

   The _____ is uppercase.
       (letter)

The English Alphabet					
Aa	Bb	Cc	Dd	Ee	Ff
Gg	Hh	Ii	Jj	Kk	Ll
Mm	Nn	Oo	Pp	Qq	Rr
Ss	Tt	Uu	Vv	Ww	Xx
Yy	Zz				

Make Observations

Look at the picture. Discuss what you see. Take notes to help you.

_____

_____

_____

_____

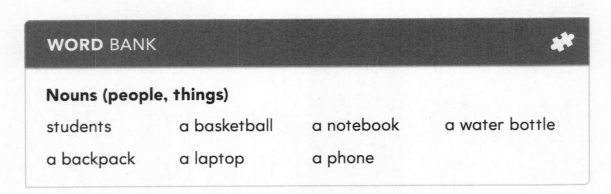

WORD BANK

Nouns (people, things)

| students | a basketball | a notebook | a water bottle |
| a backpack | a laptop | a phone | |

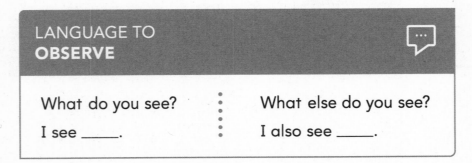

LANGUAGE TO
OBSERVE

What do you see?   What else do you see?

I see _____.   I also see _____.

Read and Respond

Read the text. Look at the first letter of each name.
Put the names in alphabetical order.

> Welcome to school! My name is **R**icardo. These are
> my friends: **O**mar, **F**atou, **A**ndi, **G**raciela, and **T**han.

A B C D E F G H I J K L M N O P Q R S T U V W X Y Z

_____

_____

_____

_____

_____

_____

WORD BANK

Names

| Omar | Fatou | Ricardo | Andi | Graciela | Than |

Write About It

> **Don't Forget!**
>
> Start names with **an uppercase letter**.
>
> **Mr. Zamora**   **Mitali**   **Los Angeles**   **English**
>
> Start sentences with **an uppercase letter**.
>
> *The alphabet has 26 letters.*
>
> Use the shift key to type an uppercase letter.

The English Alphabet

Aa	Bb	Cc	Dd	Ee	Ff
Gg	Hh	Ii	Jj	Kk	Ll
Mm	Nn	Oo	Pp	Qq	Rr
Ss	Tt	Uu	Vv	Ww	Xx
Yy	Zz				

LANGUAGE TO SHARE IDEAS

What did you write?

I wrote _____.

Complete the sentences.

1. Our teacher's name is _____.
   (Name)

   It starts with the letters _____.
   (letters)

2. Our school's name is _____.
   (Name)

   It starts with the letters _____.
   (letters)

Write Sentences

Rewrite each sentence with uppercase letters.

1. mitali and hong are friends.

_____

_____

2. my friends are enock and chen.

_____

_____

3. the teacher is mr. zamora.

_____

_____

Fantastic! Now you know all the letters in the alphabet.
Tell your partner the letter that your name begins
with: *My name begins with the letter (letter)*.

From 0 to 100

We use numbers to count or tell how many. Let's learn how to say and write numbers in English!

 Learn Numbers 0–20

Numbers 0–20

Numbers tell **how many**.

Numbers can be written using **numbers** or **words**.

number → **1   one** ← word

Listen to each number. Say each number. Count the blocks.

0	1	2	3	4	5
zero	one	two	three	four	five

6	7	8	9	10
six	seven	eight	nine	ten

11	12	13	14	15
eleven	twelve	thirteen	fourteen	fifteen

16	17	18	19	20
sixteen	seventeen	eighteen	nineteen	twenty

Language Builder

Forming Numbers 20–100

To form a **number** between 20 and 100, say the **tens** word and then the **ones** word.

tens → **25** ← ones

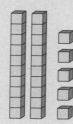

When you write numbers bigger than twenty in words, use a **hyphen** between the tens word and the ones word.

twenty-five

Listen to each number. Say each number. Count the blocks by ten.

20 twenty	
30 thirty	
40 forty	
50 fifty	
60 sixty	
70 seventy	
80 eighty	
90 ninety	
100 one hundred	

-one
-two
-three
-four
-five
-six
-seven
-eight
-nine

Listen Up

Listen to the conversation.

▶ Hello, Shaun. How many students do you see?

Hi, Taikhira! I see fifteen students.

How many teachers do you see?

I see two teachers.

How many computers do you see?

I see fifteen computers.

Talk About It

Partner A, **ask questions.** Partner B, **respond. Then switch roles.**

A: Hello! How many students do you see?

B: Hi! I see _____ students.
(number)

A: How many desks do you see?

B: I see _____ desks.
(number)

A: How many _____ do you see?
(chairs/notebooks/computers)

B: I see _____ _____.
(number)   *(chairs/notebooks/computers)*

WORD BANK

Numbers 0–20

0 zero	9 nine	18 eighteen
1 one	10 ten	19 nineteen
2 two	11 eleven	20 twenty
3 three	12 twelve	
4 four	13 thirteen	
5 five	14 fourteen	
6 six	15 fifteen	
7 seven	16 sixteen	
8 eight	17 seventeen	

Numbers by 10

10 ten
20 twenty
30 thirty
40 forty
50 fifty
60 sixty
70 seventy
80 eighty
90 ninety

Interpreting Text

 Make Observations

Look at the picture. Discuss what you see. Take notes to help you.

_____

_____

_____

_____

_____

_____

WORD BANK 🧩
Nouns (people, things)
football players   numbers
helmets   uniforms
lights

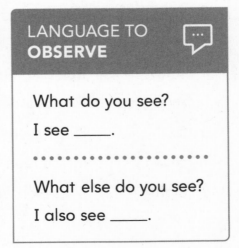

LANGUAGE TO **OBSERVE** 💬

What do you see?

I see _____.

· · · · · · · · · · · · · · · · · · · ·

What else do you see?

I also see _____.

Observe and Respond

Look at the picture to answer the questions.

1. How many football players are in the picture?

   (a) 3 football players

   (b) 7 football players

   (c) 8 football players

2. The players' uniforms have numbers on them. Which number is largest?

   (a) 80

   (b) 88

   (c) 70

3. The players' uniforms have numbers on them. Which number is smallest?

   (a) 80

   (b) 88

   (c) 70

4. Which numbers are in order from smallest to largest?

   (a) 88, 80, 70

   (b) 80, 88, 70

   (c) 70, 80, 88

Writing

Write About It

 Remember!

To write a **number** between 20 and 100, write the **tens** word and then the **ones** word. Include a hyphen between the two words.

22 → *twenty-two*

75 → *seventy-five*

WORD BANK

Numbers by 10	Numbers 0–20		
10 ten	0 zero	9 nine	18 eighteen
20 twenty	1 one	10 ten	19 nineteen
30 thirty	2 two	11 eleven	20 twenty
40 forty	3 three	12 twelve	
50 fifty	4 four	13 thirteen	
60 sixty	5 five	14 fourteen	
70 seventy	6 six	15 fifteen	
80 eighty	7 seven	16 sixteen	
90 ninety	8 eight	17 seventeen	

Count the blocks. Write the number in numbers and words.

Blocks	Numbers	Words

Write About It

Listen to each sentence. Write the missing number in numbers.

Model: Aisha is _____16_____ years old.
            (number)

1. I saw _____ students today.
         (number)

2. There are _____ teachers at this school.
             (number)

3. We need _____ computers for our class.
            (number)

WORD BANK

Numbers by 10	**Numbers 0–20**		
10 ten	0 zero	9 nine	18 eighteen
20 twenty	1 one	10 ten	19 nineteen
30 thirty	2 two	11 eleven	20 twenty
40 forty	3 three	12 twelve	
50 fifty	4 four	13 thirteen	
60 sixty	5 five	14 fourteen	
70 seventy	6 six	15 fifteen	
80 eighty	7 seven	16 sixteen	
90 ninety	8 eight	17 seventeen	

Choose one sentence to rewrite using the word for the number.

_____

_____

_____

_____

LANGUAGE TO
SHARE IDEAS

What did you write?

I wrote _____.

Good job! You just learned how to say and write numbers. Now, tell your partner a number between 20 and 100: _A number between 20 and 100 is (number)._

Vocabulary and Language

About Me

Friends want to know more about you! Let's learn how to share information about ourselves with friends and teachers.

 ### Vocabulary Builder

1. Say It   **2.** See It   **3.** Read It   **4.** Write It

---

country

coun • try
(noun)

I lived in another **country** before moving to the United States.

Word _____
   country

Translation _____

Make Connections _____

_____

---

go

go
(verb)

I **go** to Lincoln School. I am a student there.

Word _____
   go

Translation _____

Make Connections _____

_____

language

lan • guage
(noun)

The **language** I speak at home is Spanish.

Word _____
      language

Translation _____

Make Connections _____

_____

share

share
(verb)

The students **share** ideas with each other.

Word _____
      share

Translation _____

Make Connections _____

_____

years

years
(noun)

How old are you? I am 18 **years** old.

Word _____
      years

Translation _____

Make Connections _____

_____

Vocabulary Review

country	language	years
go	share	

Share translations with a partner.

**LANGUAGE TO
SHARE TRANSLATIONS**

What language do you speak?

I speak (language).

· ·

Can you share a word in (language)?

The (language) word for _____ is _____.

Complete each sentence. Then rewrite each sentence.

1. I am _____ **years** old.
(number)

_____

_____

2. I am a student. I **go** to _____.
(School Name)

_____

_____

3. I can **share** words in _____ with my partner.
(Language)

_____

_____

LANGUAGE TO COMPARE

I wrote that too.

I wrote the same answer.

 ## Language Builder

Subject Pronouns

Pronouns take the place of a person or thing. The **subject pronouns** are **I**, **you**, **he**, **she**, **it**, **we**, and **they**.

Use **I** to talk or write about yourself.

> *I speak Hmong.*

Use **you** to talk or write about someone else.

> *You speak Cantonese.*

Use **we** to talk or write about <u>a group that you are a part of</u>.

> *<u>My friends and I</u> speak Mandarin.*
> *We speak Mandarin.*

Use **he**, **she**, or **they** to talk or write about <u>other people</u>.

> *<u>Omar</u> speaks Arabic. **He** speaks Arabic.*
>
> *<u>Aisha</u> speaks Somali. **She** speaks Somali.*
>
> *<u>Mitali</u> speaks English. **They** speak English.*
>
> *<u>Graciela and Ricardo</u> speak Spanish.*
> *They speak Spanish.*

Use **it** to talk or write about <u>one thing</u>.

> *<u>The book</u> is on the desk. **It** is on the desk.*

Highlight the pronoun that takes the place of the <u>underlined</u> subject.

Model: <u>Ms. Santos</u> is a teacher. She is a teacher.

1. <u>Caleb</u> is from Texas. He is from Texas.

2. <u>The computer</u> is on the desk. It is on the desk.

3. <u>Lina and I</u> go to City Middle School. We go to City Middle School.

4. <u>The new student</u> is 13 years old. They are 13 years old.

> **LANGUAGE TO SHARE IDEAS** 💬
>
> What did you highlight?
>
> I highlighted the pronoun _____.

Write the correct pronoun to take the place of the <u>underlined</u> subject.

Model: <u>Mr. Liu</u> teaches English. _____He_____ teaches English.
(Pronoun)

1. <u>Peter and Alejandro</u> are 16 years old. _____ are 16 years old.
(Pronoun)

2. <u>Ms. Amin</u> speaks Arabic. _____ speaks Arabic.
(Pronoun)

3. <u>My friends and I</u> go to Village High School.

_____ go to Village High School.
(Pronoun)

4. <u>The desk</u> is big.

_____ is big.
(Pronoun)

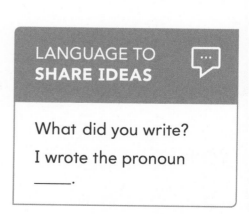

> **LANGUAGE TO SHARE IDEAS** 💬
>
> What did you write?
>
> I wrote the pronoun _____.

Listen Up

Listen to the conversation.

▶ Hello, Serene! Could you tell me about yourself? How old are you?

Sure, Mateo! I am 16 years old.

Where are you from?

I am from Algeria.

Wow! What languages do you speak?

I speak French and Arabic.

Talk About It

Partner A, **ask questions. Partner B,** respond. **Then switch roles.**

A: Hello, _____! Could you tell me
       (Name)

   about yourself? How old are you?

B: I am _____ years old.
       (number)

A: Where are you from?

B: I am from _____.
              (Country)

A: Wow! What languages do you speak?

B: I speak _____
              (Language)

   and _____.
        (Language)

Read the word bank. Add languages.

WORD BANK

Languages		Numbers 8–21	
Arabic	Portuguese	8 eight	15 fifteen
Cantonese	Russian	9 nine	16 sixteen
English	Somali	10 ten	17 seventeen
Haitian Creole	Spanish	11 eleven	18 eighteen
Hmong	Tagalog	12 twelve	19 nineteen
Mandarin	Vietnamese	13 thirteen	20 twenty
_____		14 fourteen	21 twenty-one

Text Type: Poem

A **poem** uses **descriptive language** to explore ideas and feelings. The **poet**, or **author**, is the person who wrote the poem. The **speaker** is the voice of the poem.

Bilingual

by Alma Flor Ada

Because I speak Spanish
I can listen to my grandmother's stories
and say familia, madre, amor.
Because I speak English
5   I can learn from my teacher
and say *I love school*.
Because I am bilingual
I can read *libros* and *books*,
I have *amigos* and *friends*,
10   **enjoy** *canciones* and *songs*,
juegos and *games*
and have **twice as much** fun.
And someday,
because I speak two **languages**,
15   I will be able to do twice as much
to help twice as many people
and be twice as good in what I do.

Glossary

....

familia
Familia in Spanish is *family* in English.

madre
Madre in Spanish is *mother* in English.

amor
Amor in Spanish is *love* in English.

enjoy (verb)
Enjoy means *like*.

twice as much
Twice as much means *double*.

Bilingüe

por Alma Flor Ada

Porque hablo español

puedo escuchar los cuentos de abuelita

y decir *familia*, *madre*, *amor*.

Porque hablo inglés

5   puedo aprender de mi maestra

y decir *I love school*.

Porque soy bilingüe

puedo leer *libros* y *books*,

tengo *amigos* y *friends*,

10   disfruto *canciones* y *songs*,

juegos y *games*

¡y me divierto el doble!

Y algún día,

porque hablo dos idiomas,

15   podré hacer doble esfuerzo

para ayudar al doble de personas

y lo haré todo el doble de bien.

Take notes on the poem.

_____

_____

_____

_____

LANGUAGE TO REACT

Did you enjoy the poem?

Yes, I enjoyed the poem.

No, I did not enjoy the poem.

. . . .

What question do you have about the poem?

One question I have is: ____?

Identify Repetition

> **Repetition**
>
> Some poems have **repetition**, or words or phrases that are used over and over.

Reread the poem. Highlight words or phrases that repeat.

Bilingual
by Alma Flor Ada

Because I speak Spanish

I can listen to my grandmother's stories

and say *familia*, *madre*, *amor*.

Because I speak English

5 I can learn from my teacher

and say *I love school*.

Because I am bilingual

I can read *libros* and *books*,

I have *amigos* and *friends*,

10 enjoy *canciones* and *songs*,

juegos and *games*

and have twice as much fun.

And someday,

because I speak two languages,

15 I will be able to do twice as much

to help twice as many people

and be twice as good in what I do.

 ## Read and Respond

Reread the poem. <u>Underline</u> things the speaker can do. Then answer the questions.

1. Reread lines 7 to 12 in the poem. Why does the poet use the same words in Spanish and in English?

    (a) She wants the reader to know the translation of those words.

    (b) She wants to show that these are things the speaker does in both Spanish and English.

    (c) She wants to show that the speaker does everything twice, first in Spanish, then in English.

2. Reread lines 7 to 12 in the poem. Why does the speaker say they have "twice as much fun"?

    (a) They like doing everything two times.

    (b) They can do everything in two languages.

    (c) They have twice as many books, friends, songs, and games.

Write About It

> **Don't forget!**
>
> Use **I** to talk or write about yourself.
>
> *I speak Hmong.*
>
> Use **we** to talk or write about <u>a group that you are a part of</u>.
>
> *<u>My friends and I</u> speak English.* **We** *speak English.*
>
> Use **he**, **she**, or **they** to talk or write about <u>other people</u>.
>
> *<u>Omar</u> speaks Arabic.* **He** *speaks Arabic.*
>
> *<u>Aisha</u> speaks Somali.* **She** *speaks Somali.*
>
> *<u>Mitali</u> speaks English.* **They** *speak English.*
>
> *<u>Graciela and Ricardo</u> speak Spanish.* **They** *speak Spanish.*

WORD BANK

Numbers 8–21

8 eight	15 fifteen
9 nine	16 sixteen
10 ten	17 seventeen
11 eleven	18 eighteen
12 twelve	19 nineteen
13 thirteen	20 twenty
14 fourteen	21 twenty-one

Languages

Arabic	Portuguese
Cantonese	Russian
English	Somali
Haitian Creole	Spanish
Hmong	Tagalog
Mandarin	Vietnamese
	_____

Write about yourself.

Model:

My name is <u>Edwin</u>.

I am <u>15</u> years old.

I am from <u>Colombia</u>.

I speak <u>Spanish</u> and <u>English</u>.

My name is _____ .

                  (Name)

_____ am _____ years old.

(Pronoun)   *(number)*

_____ am from _____ .

(Pronoun)   *(Country)*

_____ speak _____

(Pronoun)   *(Language)*

and _____ .

     (Language)

Write your sentences.

_____

_____

_____

_____

_____

Writing

 **Ask and Write**

Interview a classmate. Take notes.

Question	Answer
What is your name?	
What are your pronouns?	
How old are you?	
Where are you from?	
What languages do you speak?	
Where do you go to school?	

WORD BANK

Numbers 8–21

8 eight	15 fifteen
9 nine	16 sixteen
10 ten	17 seventeen
11 eleven	18 eighteen
12 twelve	19 nineteen
13 thirteen	20 twenty
14 fourteen	21 twenty-one

Languages

Arabic	Portuguese
Cantonese	Russian
English	Somali
Haitian Creole	Spanish
Hmong	Tagalog
Mandarin	Vietnamese

Write sentences about your classmate.

Model:

My classmate's name is Joy.

Joy is sixteen years old.

She is from Haiti.

Joy speaks Haitian Creole and English.

We go to school at Smith High School.

My classmate's name is _____ .
            (Name)

_____ is _____ years old.
            (Name)   (number)

_____ from _____ .
(He is/She is/They are)   (Country)

_____ speaks _____
            (Name)   (Language)
and _____ .
        (Language)

_____ go to school at _____ .
    (Pronoun)   (School Name)

Terrific! You just learned how to share information about yourself. Now, tell your partner one thing about yourself: *One thing about me is that I (verb phrase)*.

People at School

At school, you meet teachers, students, and many other people! Let's learn about the people at school.

 Vocabulary Builder

1. Say It   **2.** See It   **3.** Read It   **4.** Write It

---

principal

prin • ci • pal
(noun)

The **principal** leads the school.

Word _____
       principal

Translation _____

Make Connections _____

_____

---

assistant

as • **sis** • tant
(noun)

An **assistant** helps the principal and teachers.

Word _____
       assistant

Translation _____

Make Connections _____

_____

coach

coach
(noun)

The **coach** teaches gym class and sports.

Word _____
       coach

Translation _____

Make Connections _____

_____

counselor

coun • sel • or
(noun)

A **counselor** gives advice to students.

Word _____
       counselor

Translation _____

Make Connections _____

_____

custodian

cus • **to** • di • an
(noun)

A **custodian** cleans and fixes things in the school.

Word _____
       custodian

Translation _____

Make Connections _____

_____

food service worker

food **ser** • vice **work** • er
(noun)

A **food service worker** makes and serves food at school.

Word _____
      food service worker

Translation _____

Make Connections _____

_____

librarian

li • **brar** • i • an
(noun)

The **librarian** helps students find books in the library.

Word _____
      librarian

Translation _____

Make Connections _____

_____

nurse

nurse
(noun)

The **nurse** gives medical care to students.

Word _____
      nurse

Translation _____

Make Connections _____

_____

Vocabulary Review

principal	counselor	librarian
assistant	custodian	nurse
coach	food service worker	

Share translations with a partner.

> **LANGUAGE TO SHARE TRANSLATIONS** 💬
>
> Can you share a word in (language)?
> The (language) word for _____ is _____.

Who are other important people at your school?

These are other important people at my school:

- _____

- _____

- _____

- _____

- _____

Language Builder

Nouns for People

Nouns are words for people, places, things, and ideas.

A **noun for a person** tells **who** someone is.

> *principal   librarian   nurse*

A **common noun** starts with a <u>lowercase letter</u>.

> The **_principal_** *is Ms. Tate.*

Names are **proper nouns**. They start with <u>an uppercase letter</u>.

> *The principal is* **_Ms. Tate_**.

Highlight the nouns for people. <u>Underline</u> the proper nouns.

Model: A librarian helps students find books. The librarian is <u>Ms. Musa</u>.

1. A counselor gives advice.

2. The counselor is Mr. Gomez.

3. A custodian cleans and fixes things.

4. The custodian is Mr. Jones.

5. A food service worker makes and serves food.

6. The food service worker is Ms. Amin.

7. A nurse gives medical care.

8. The nurse is Ms. Petro.

LANGUAGE TO
SHARE IDEAS

What did you highlight?
I highlighted _____.

What did you underline?
I underlined _____.

Listen Up

Listen to the conversation.

 Hi, Chris! Who gives advice to students at school?

Hello, Maria! A counselor gives advice to students.

Who gives medical care to students at school?

A school nurse gives medical care to students.

Talk About It

Partner A, **ask questions.** Partner B, **respond. Then switch roles.**

A: Hi, _____!
(Name)

Who helps students find books in the library?

B: Hello, _____.
(Name)

A _____ helps students find books.
(noun)

A: Thanks! Who makes and serves food at school?

B: A _____
(noun)

makes and serves food at school.

A: Thanks, _____! Who teaches sports?
(Name)

B: A _____ teaches sports.
(noun)

WORD BANK		
Nouns (people)		
assistant	custodian	nurse
coach	food service worker	principal
counselor	librarian	

Make Observations

Look at the pictures. Discuss what you see. Take notes to help you.

principal

counselor

librarian

custodian

_____

_____

_____

_____

food service worker

nurse

coach

assistant

_____

_____

_____

_____

LANGUAGE TO **OBSERVE**

Who do you see?

I see _____.

Who else do you see?

I also see _____.

Read and Respond

Read the text. Then answer the questions.

principal

counselor

librarian

custodian

food service worker

nurse

coach

assistant

Many people work at Amir's school. The **principal** is Ms. Tate. She is the leader of the school. Mr. Gomez is the **counselor**. He gives advice to students. The **librarian** is Ms. Musa. She helps students find books. Mr. Jones is a **custodian**. He cleans and fixes things. Ms. Amin, a **food service worker**, makes and serves food. The **nurse**, Ms. Petro, gives medical care to students. The **coach** is Ms. Kaya. She teaches students to play basketball, softball, and other sports. The **assistant** is Ms. Kelly. She works with the principal.

1. Who leads a school?

   The _____ leads a school.
   (noun)

2. Who gives advice to students?

   A _____ gives advice to students.
   (noun)

3. What does a librarian do?

   A librarian _____.
   (verb phrase)

4. What does a custodian do?

   A custodian _____.
   (verb phrase)

5. What does a _____ do?
   (noun)

   _____
   (verb phrase)

WORD BANK

Nouns (people)		Verb Phrases (action phrases)
assistant	food service worker	cleans and fixes things
coach	librarian	helps students find books
counselor	nurse	makes and serves food
custodian	principal	teaches students to play sports

Write About It

 Remember!

Names are **proper nouns**. A **proper noun** starts with an <u>uppercase letter</u>.

The coach is **<u>Ms. Kaya</u>**.

Write sentences about the people at your school.

Model: Who cleans and fixes things? The ____custodian____ cleans and fixes things.
(noun)

Who is the custodian? The custodian is _____.
(Proper Noun)

1. Who leads the school? The _____ leads the school.
(noun)

Who is the principal? The principal is _____.
(Proper Noun)

2. Who helps students find books? The _____
(noun)

helps students find books.

Who is the librarian? The librarian is _____.
(Proper Noun)

3. Who gives advice to students? The _____
(noun)

gives advice to students.

Who is the counselor? The counselor is _____.
(Proper Noun)

WORD BANK

Nouns (people)

assistant	food service worker
coach	librarian
counselor	nurse
custodian	principal

LANGUAGE TO **COMPARE**

I wrote that too.

I wrote the same answer.

Great work! You just learned the names of people at school. Now, tell a partner about someone who has helped you at school: *Someone who has helped me at school is (Name). (Pronoun) is (the/my) (noun for a person).*

School Supplies

Students need different items to help them learn at school. Let's learn the names for school supplies.

 ### Vocabulary Builder

1. Say It   **2.** See It   **3.** Read It   **4.** Write It

backpack
back • pack
(noun)

I carry my supplies in my **backpack**.

Word _____
      backpack

Translation _____

Make Connections _____

_____

book
book
(noun)

I read a **book** in school.

Word _____
      book

Translation _____

Make Connections _____

_____

calculator

cal • cu • **la** • tor
(noun)

I use a **calculator** to help me in math class.

Word _____
        calculator

Translation _____

Make Connections _____

_____

computer

com • **put** • er
(noun)

I use a **computer** in my class.

Word _____
        computer

Translation _____

Make Connections _____

_____

folder

fold • er
(noun)

I use a **folder** to hold my papers.

Word _____
        folder

Translation _____

Make Connections _____

_____

Vocabulary and Language

notebook

note • book
(noun)

I take notes in my **notebook**.

Word _____
   notebook

Translation _____

Make Connections _____

_____

pen

pen
(noun)

I use my **pen** to write.

Word _____
   pen

Translation _____

Make Connections _____

_____

pencil

pen • cil
(noun)

I take notes with a **pencil**.

Word _____
   pencil

Translation _____

Make Connections _____

_____

Vocabulary Review

backpack	computer	pen
book	folder	pencil
calculator	notebook	

Share translations with a partner.

> **LANGUAGE TO SHARE TRANSLATIONS**
>
> Can you share a word in (language)?
>
> The (language) word for _____ is _____.

What other school supplies do you need?

These are other supplies I need at school:

- _____
- _____
- _____
- _____
- _____

Language Builder

Nouns for Things

Nouns are words for people, places, things, and ideas.

A **noun for a thing** refers to an **object**.

book   pen   folder

A **singular noun** refers to one person, place, thing, or idea.

a teacher   the school   a book

A **plural noun** refers to more than one person, place, thing, or idea. Add **–s** to form a plural noun.

a teacher → **three teacher_s_**

the school → **many school_s_**

a book → **10 book_s_**

When a singular noun ends in **–s**, **–z**, **–x**, **–sh**, or **–ch**, add **–es** to form the **plural noun**.

one class → **many class_es_**

1. Write the correct noun under each image.

_____   _____

pen	pens

2. Write the correct noun under each image.

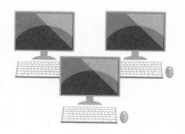

_____   _____

| computer | computers |

3. Write the correct noun under each image.

_____   _____

| backpack | backpacks |

Write the correct noun.

1. I need a _____ to write.
(pencil/pencils)

2. I need two _____: one for math and one for English.
(notebooks/notebook)

3. The class has 11 students, so we need 11 _____.
(folder/folders)

Listen Up

Listen to the conversation.

 Hi, Shaun! What school supplies do I need for class?

Hello, Taikhira! For class, you need a notebook.

Thank you for your help. What else do I need?

You also need a pen or a pencil.

I don't have a pencil. Could I borrow one?

Sure, you can borrow one!

Talk About It

Partner A, **ask questions.** Partner B, **respond. Then switch roles.**

A: Hi, _____!
    (Name)

   What do I need for class?

B: Hello, _____!
    (Name)

   For class, you need a _____.
                          (noun)

A: What else do I need?

B: You also need a _____.
                    (noun)

A: I don't have a _____. Could I borrow one?
                   (noun)

B: Sure, you can borrow one!

WORD BANK   ✦

Nouns (things)

backpack   computer   pen

book   folder   pencil

calculator   notebook

Interpreting Media

Listen and Respond

Listen to the teacher read a list of supplies that students need for school.

Take notes on the supplies students need for school.

Topic: School Supplies List

- _____ notebooks

- _____ pens

- 10 _____

- _____

- _____

WORD BANK

Nouns (things)

backpack   calculator   notebooks   pencils   pens

Answer the questions.

1. How many notebooks do students need?

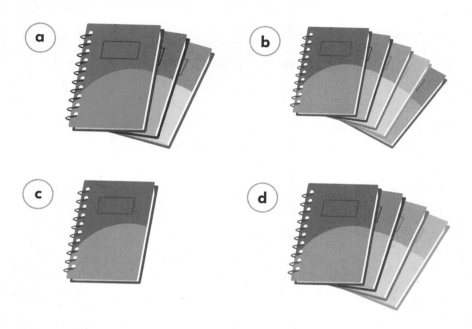

2. What do students need to carry their supplies?

Write About It

 Don't Forget!

Use a **plural noun** when there is more than one of something.
Add **–s** or **–es** to form a plural noun.

one pencil → **ten pencils**

Write how many of each supply you need for school.
Add **–s** to the noun if you need more than one.

My School Supplies

(number)	(calculator)
(number)	(pen)
(number)	(pencil)
(number)	(book)
(number)	(computer)
(number)	(notebook)
(number)	(backpack)
(number)	(folder)

WORD BANK

Numbers 1–10

1 one	3 three	5 five	7 seven	9 nine
2 two	4 four	6 six	8 eight	10 ten

Write sentences to tell what you need for school every day.

Model: I need _____one_____ _____calculator_____ to solve math problems.
            (number)   *(noun)*

1. I need _____ _____
              (number)   *(noun)*

    to _____.
      (verb phrase)

2. I need _____ _____
              (number)   *(noun)*

    to _____.
      (verb phrase)

3. I need _____ _____
              (number)   *(noun)*

    to _____.
      (verb phrase)

WORD BANK

Verb Phrases (action phrases)

| carry my school supplies | hold my papers |
| help me learn | take notes |

LANGUAGE TO **SHARE IDEAS**

What did you write?

I wrote _____.

Well done! You just learned all about school supplies. Now, tell your partner one school supply you use every day: *I use a (noun) every day.*

Class Acts

Students do many things at school, like read and write. Let's learn about other important actions that happen at school!

 ## Vocabulary Builder

1. Say It   **2.** See It   **3.** Read It   **4.** Write It

find
find
(verb)

Laura can **find** a teacher to help her.

Word _____
    find

Translation _____

Make Connections _____

_____

hang out
hang out
(verb)

Fatou **hangs out** with her friends at lunch.

Word _____
    hang out

Translation _____

Make Connections _____

_____

learn

learn
(verb)

I **learn** many things at school.

Word _____
       learn

Translation _____

Make Connections _____

_____

play

play
(verb)

We **play** volleyball at school.

Word _____
       play

Translation _____

Make Connections _____

_____

practice

prac • tice
(verb)

I **practice** basketball after school.

Word _____
       practice

Translation _____

Make Connections _____

_____

solve

solve
(verb)

He can **solve** the math problem.

Word _____
       solve

Translation _____

Make Connections _____

_____

study

stud • y
(verb)

I **study** vocabulary after school.

Word _____
       study

Translation _____

Make Connections _____

_____

understand

un • der • stand
(verb)

Samira **understands** two languages.

Word _____
       understand

Translation _____

Make Connections _____

_____

Vocabulary Review

find	play	study
hang out	practice	understand
learn	solve	

Share translations with a partner.

> **LANGUAGE TO**
> **SHARE TRANSLATIONS** 💬
>
> Can you share a word in (language)?
> The (language) word for _____ is _____.

What other actions do you do at school?

These are other actions I do at school:

- _____

- _____

- _____

- _____

- _____

Language Builder

Present-Tense Verbs

A **verb** is an **action word**, like *read* or *write*.

I **read** books at school.

A **present-tense verb** tells what is happening right now or all the time. Regular **present-tense verbs** change depending on the <u>subject</u>, the person doing the action.

<u>I</u> **read** books.

<u>You</u> **read** books.

<u>He/She/It</u> **read<u>s</u>** books.

<u>My friend</u> **read<u>s</u>** books.

<u>Leo</u> **read<u>s</u>** books.

<u>We</u> **read** books.

<u>They</u> **read** books.

Underline the verbs.

Model: I <u>practice</u> English every day.

1. I learn new information from my teacher.

2. We study vocabulary in English class.

3. Mateo understands two languages.

4. They solve math problems in math class.

5. Damsa hangs out with her new friends.

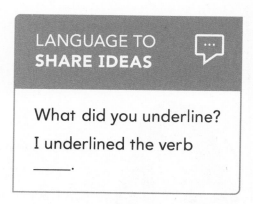

LANGUAGE TO
SHARE IDEAS

What did you underline?

I underlined the verb

_____.

Write the correct form of the present-tense verb *practice* **in each sentence.**

Model: Rian _____practices_____ new words on his phone.
          (verb)

1. I _____ new words in English class.
    (verb)

2. Marisa _____ new words with her partner.
      (verb)

3. We _____ new words on the computer.
    (verb)

LANGUAGE TO
SHARE IDEAS

What did you write?

I wrote _____.

Speaking and Listening

 Listen Up

Listen to the conversation.

 Hello, Serene! What do you do at school?

Hello, Mateo! I play soccer and read books at school.

Cool! What else do you do at school?

I also hang out with friends and practice English.

Talk About It

Partner A, ask questions. Partner B, respond. Then switch roles.

A: Hello, _____!
             (Name)
   What do you do at school?

B: Hello, _____!
             (Name)
   I _____ at school.
   (verb phrase)

A: Interesting. What else do you do at school?

B: I also _____ and
          (verb phrase)
   _____ at school.
   (verb phrase)

WORD BANK

Verb Phrases (action phrases)

ask questions	play soccer	solve math problems
hang out with friends	practice English	study science
learn new words	read books	_____

Text Type: Speech

A **speech** is said aloud to an audience. The **speaker** gives, or says, the speech. The **audience** listens to the speaker.

Former President Barack Obama gives a speech to students.

President Obama Speaks to America's Students

September 8, 2009
Wakefield High School; Arlington, Virginia

1   No one's born being good at all things. You become good at things through hard work. You're not a varsity athlete the first time you **play** a new sport. You don't hit every note the first time you sing a song. You've got to **practice**. The same principle applies to your schoolwork. You might have to do a math problem a few times before you get it right. You might have to read something a few times before you **understand** it. You definitely have to do a few drafts of a paper before it's good enough to hand in.

2   Don't be afraid to ask questions. Don't be afraid to ask for help when you need it. I do that every day. Asking for help isn't a sign of weakness. It's a sign of strength because it shows you have the courage to admit when you don't know something, and that then allows you to **learn** something new. So **find** an adult that you trust—a parent, a grandparent or teacher, a coach or a counselor—and ask them to help you stay on track to meet your goals.

Glossary

few (adjective)
If you do something a *few* times, you do it more than once.

afraid (adjective)
When someone is *afraid*, they are scared or nervous.

courage (noun)
Courage is the ability to do something difficult.

Take notes on the speech.

_____

_____

_____

_____

_____

_____

_____

LANGUAGE TO REACT

Did you enjoy the speech?

Yes, I enjoyed the speech.
No, I did not enjoy the speech.

What question do you have about the speech?

One question I have is: _____?

Read and Respond

> **Main Idea**
>
> The **main idea** is the most important idea in a text or paragraph.

Read the speech again. <u>Underline</u> the main idea in each paragraph.

President Obama Speaks to America's Students

September 8, 2009
Wakefield High School; Arlington, Virginia

1   No one's born being good at all things. You become good at things through hard work. You're not a varsity athlete the first time you **play** a new sport. You don't hit every note the first time you sing a song. You've got to **practice**. The same principle applies to your schoolwork. You might have to do a math problem a few times before you get it right. You might have to read something a few times before you **understand** it. You definitely have to do a few drafts of a paper before it's good enough to hand in.

2   Don't be afraid to ask questions. Don't be afraid to ask for help when you need it. I do that every day. Asking for help isn't a sign of weakness. It's a sign of strength because it shows you have the courage to admit when you don't know something, and that then allows you to **learn** something new. So **find** an adult that you trust—a parent, a grandparent or teacher, a coach or a counselor—and ask them to help you stay on track to meet your goals.

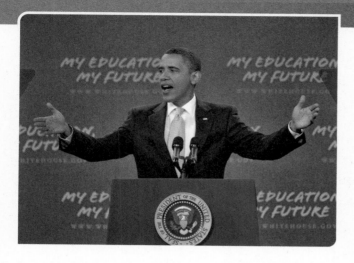

Write each main idea in your own words. Then write a summary.

Main Idea 1: You become good at things through hard work.

In Your Words: You learn through _____ .

(noun)

Main Idea 2: Don't be afraid to ask for help when you need it.

In Your Words: You need to _____ for help.

(verb)

Summary: The main idea of the text is that we learn through

_____ and

(noun)

we need to _____ for help.

(verb)

Read and Respond

Answer the questions about the text.

1. President Obama said, "You might have to read something a few times before you understand it."

   Which picture shows this idea?

a

b

c

d

2. Reread this section of the speech.

"Don't be afraid to ask for help when you need it. I do that every day. Asking for help isn't a sign of weakness. It's a sign of strength because it shows you have the courage to admit when you don't know something, and that then allows you to learn something new."

What does President Obama do every day?

(a) He gives a speech.

(b) He writes a paper.

(c) He asks for help.

3. Reread this section of the speech.

"Don't be afraid to ask for help when you need it. I do that every day. Asking for help isn't a sign of weakness. It's a sign of strength because it shows you have the courage to admit when you don't know something, and that then allows you to learn something new."

Why is it important to ask for help?

(a) It means you are afraid.

(b) It is a sign of weakness.

(c) It can help you learn something new.

Writing

 Write About It

> **Remember!**
>
> After *I*, use the **base form** of a verb for the present tense.
>
> *I **study** new words.*
>
> The base form of a verb has no ending, such as **–s** or **–ing**.

Read each verb. Write a noun to tell about an action you do at school.

ask _____

hang out with _____

learn _____

play _____

practice _____

read _____

speak _____

study _____

LANGUAGE TO SHARE IDEAS

What did you write?

I wrote ____.

· ·

What else did you write?

I also wrote ____.

WORD BANK

Nouns (people, things, ideas)

books	friends	questions	Spanish
classmates	math	science	sports
English			

President Obama said, "Don't be afraid to ask for help when you need it. I do that every day."

Write sentences to tell what you do at school every day.

Model: I _____ask questions_____ at school every day.

1. I _____ at school every day.

2. I _____ at school every day.

3. I also _____ at school every day.

Write a paragraph to tell what you do at school every day.

I do many things at school every day. I _____.
                                        (verb phrase)

I _____.
  (verb phrase)

I _____, and
  (verb phrase)

I _____.
  (verb phrase)

I also _____.
     (verb phrase)

Great job! You just learned about actions at school. Now, tell your partner one thing you do at school: *At school, I (verb phrase)*.

Places at School

Students go to many different places at school. Let's learn the names of places so you know where you need to go.

 ## Vocabulary Builder

1. Say It   **2.** See It   **3.** Read It   **4.** Write It

---

bathroom
bath • room
(noun)

A student washes his hands in the **bathroom**.

Word _____
     bathroom

Translation _____

Make Connections _____

_____

---

cafeteria
caf • e • **te** • ri •a
(noun)

Students eat breakfast and lunch in the **cafeteria**.

Word _____
     cafeteria

Translation _____

Make Connections _____

_____

classroom

class • room
(noun)

Students learn in the **classroom**.

Word _____
classroom

Translation _____

Make Connections _____

_____

gym

gym
(noun)

Students play sports like basketball in the **gym**.

Word _____
gym

Translation _____

Make Connections _____

_____

hallway

hall • way
(noun)

Students walk in the **hallway**.

Word _____
hallway

Translation _____

Make Connections _____

_____

library

li • brar • y
(noun)

A student reads in the **library**.

Word _____
    library

Translation _____

Make Connections _____

_____

office

of • fice
(noun)

The principal works in the **office**.

Word _____
    office

Translation _____

Make Connections _____

_____

schoolyard

school • yard
(noun)

Students hang out in the **schoolyard**.

Word _____
    schoolyard

Translation _____

Make Connections _____

_____

Vocabulary Review

bathroom	gym	office
cafeteria	hallway	schoolyard
classroom	library	

Share translations with a partner.

> **LANGUAGE TO SHARE TRANSLATIONS**
>
> Can you share a word in (language)?
> The (language) word for _____ is _____.

What are other places at your school?

These are other places at my school:

- _____

- _____

- _____

- _____

- _____

Language Builder

Nouns for Places

Nouns are words for people, places, things, and ideas.

A **noun for place** tells **where something happens**.

> classroom   hallway   gym

Use <u>in the</u> before the place to tell where something happens at school.

> Students walk <u>in the</u> **hallway**.

> Students hang out <u>in the</u> **schoolyard**.

Highlight nouns for places at school.
<u>Underline</u> *in the* before the place at school.

Model: Students walk <u>in the</u> hallway.

1. Students learn in the classroom.

2. The principal works in the main office.

3. Students play sports in the gym.

4. Students eat breakfast and lunch in the cafeteria.

5. A teacher washes her hands in the bathroom.

> **LANGUAGE TO
> SHARE IDEAS**
>
> What did you highlight?
> I highlighted _____.

Listen Up

Listen to the conversation.

 Hello, Chris! Where do students eat lunch?

Hi, Maria! Students eat lunch in the cafeteria.

Thanks! Where is the principal, Ms. Mosby?

The principal works in the main office. I can show you where it is.

Talk About It

Partner A, **ask questions. Partner B, respond. Then switch roles.**

A: Hello, _____ !
        (Name)

Where do students learn?

B: Hi, _____ .
       (Name)

Students learn in the _____ .
                        (noun)

A: Thanks! Where do students play sports?

B: Students play sports in the _____ .
                                 (noun)

A: Where do students _____ ?
                       (verb phrase)

B: Students _____ in
              (verb phrase)

the _____ .
      (noun)

WORD BANK

Nouns (places)		**Verb Phrases (action phrases)**	
bathroom	hallway	eat lunch	talk to the principal
cafeteria	library	hang out with friends	wash their hands
classroom	office	read books	
gym	schoolyard		

Interpreting Text

 ## Make Observations

Look at the picture. Discuss what you see. Take notes to help you.

_____

_____

_____

_____

_____

_____

_____

WORD BANK

Nouns (people)

a coach	a teacher	the nurse
a food service worker	an assistant	the principal
a librarian	the counselor	students

LANGUAGE TO OBSERVE

What do you see?	What else do you see?
I see ____ in the ____.	I also see ____ in the ____.

Read and Respond

Read the text. Then answer the questions.

Students go to many different places at school. They eat in the **cafeteria**. They study in the **classrooms**, computer lab, and **library**. They play sports outside and in the **gym**. They go to the **office** to ask the nurse and the counselor for help. There are many places to go at school.

1. Where do students eat? Students eat in the _____.

2. Where do students study? Students study in the _____, computer lab, and _____.

3. Where do students play sports? Students play sports outside and in the _____.

4. Where is the counselor? The counselor is in the _____.

WORD BANK ✦
Nouns (places)

bathroom	gym	office
cafeteria	hallway	schoolyard
classroom	library	

Write About It

> **Don't forget!**
>
> Use <u>in the</u> **(place)** to talk about **where** something happens at school.
>
> *Students read <u>in the</u> **library**.*
>
> *Students eat <u>in the</u> **cafeteria**.*

WORD BANK		
Nouns (places)		**Nouns (people)**
bathroom	hallway	counselor
cafeteria	library	principal
classroom	office	students
gym	schoolyard	teacher

Write sentences to tell where things happen at your school.

Model: Where do students walk?

Students walk <u>in the hallway</u>.
in the + (noun for place)

1. Where do students play sports?

   Students play sports _____.
   in the + (noun for place)

2. Where do students learn?

   Students learn _____.
   in the + (noun for place)

3. Where do students eat lunch?

   _____ eat lunch _____.
   (Noun for People) *in the + (noun for place)*

4. Where does the principal work?

   The _____ works _____.
   (noun for person) *in the + (noun for place)*

5. Where do students hang out?

   _____.

Bravo! You just learned the names of places at school. Now, tell your partner where you like to hang out with friends at school: *I like to hang out with friends in the (noun).*

School Subjects

At school, students learn about many subjects, like science or art. Let's learn the names of the subjects you learn about in school!

 Vocabulary Builder

1. Say It   **2.** See It   **3.** Read It   **4.** Write It

subject

sub • ject
(noun)

A school **subject** is a topic you study in school.

Word _____
  subject

Translation _____

Make Connections _____

_____

English

Eng • lish
(noun)

In **English** class, students read and write in **English**.

Word _____
  English

Translation _____

Make Connections _____

_____

math

math
(noun)

In **math**, students use numbers to solve problems.

Word _____
      math

Translation _____

Make Connections _____

_____

science

sci • ence
(noun)

Students study nature in **science**.

Word _____
      science

Translation _____

Make Connections _____

_____

social studies

so • cial **stud** • ies
(noun)

Students use maps in **social studies**.

Word _____
      social studies

Translation _____

Make Connections _____

_____

Vocabulary and Language

art

art
(noun)

Students draw and paint in **art**.

Word _____
　　　　art

Translation _____

Make Connections _____

_____

physical education

phys • i • cal
ed • u • ca • tion
(noun)

Students play sports in **physical education**, or P.E.

Word _____
　　　　physical education

Translation _____

Make Connections _____

_____

favorite

fa • vor • ite
(adjective)

Her **favorite** subject is science because she likes to do experiments.

Word _____
　　　　favorite

Translation _____

Make Connections _____

_____

Vocabulary Review

subject	science	physical education
English	social studies	favorite
math	art	

Share translations with a partner.

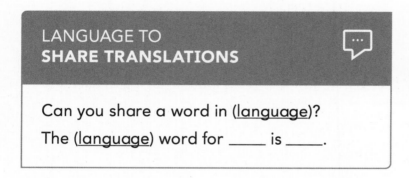

LANGUAGE TO
SHARE TRANSLATIONS

Can you share a word in (language)?
The (language) word for _____ is _____.

What other classes are taught at this school?

This school has many other classes:

- _____

- _____

- _____

- _____

- _____

Language Builder

Nouns for Ideas

Nouns are words for people, places, things, and ideas.

A **noun for an idea** is an **abstract noun**, a word for something that we cannot see or touch.

education   *laughter*   *science*

WORD BANK

Nouns (people, places, things, ideas)

bathroom	counselor	office
book	desk	principal
coach	education	science lab
computer	language	social studies

LANGUAGE TO COLLABORATE

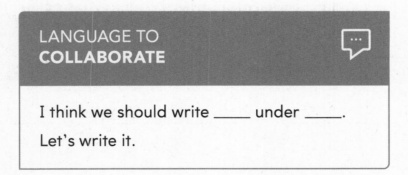

I think we should write _____ under _____.

Let's write it.

Sort the nouns into people, places, things, and ideas.

People	Places	Things	Ideas

LANGUAGE TO REPORT IDEAS

We wrote the nouns _____, _____, and _____ under (<u>category</u>).

Listen Up

Listen to the conversation.

 Hi, Shaun! What is your favorite subject?

Hello, Taikhira! My favorite subject is social studies.

Why is social studies your favorite subject?

I like to learn about history.

Talk About It

Partner A, **ask questions. Partner B, respond. Then switch roles.**

A: Hi, _____ ! What is your favorite subject?
       (Name)

B: Hello, _____ ! My favorite subject
          (Name)

   is _____.
    (noun)

A: Why is that your favorite subject?

B: I like to _____.
    (verb phrase)

Listen and take notes.

Classmate's Name	
Favorite Subject	

WORD BANK

Nouns (ideas)		Verb Phrases (action phrases)	
art	physical education	do experiments	play sports
English	science	draw pictures	read books
math	social studies	learn about history	solve math problems
_____			

Reading a Bar Graph

A **bar graph** uses bars to show how many are in each group or category.

To read a bar graph:

1. Find a group. Put your finger on the bar.

2. Move your finger to the top of the bar.

3. Move your finger to the left to find the number or amount for that group.

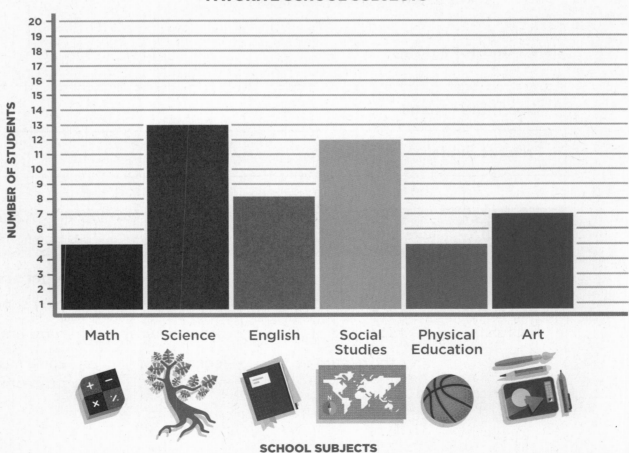

FAVORITE SCHOOL SUBJECTS

Read and Respond

Read the bar graph to answer the questions.

1. What is the title of the graph?
The title of the graph is _____.

     (a) School Subjects

     (b) Number of Students

     (c) Favorite School Subjects

2. How many students said their favorite school subject is math?
_____ students said their favorite school subject is math.

     (a) 5

     (b) 10

     (c) 15

3. How many students said their favorite school subject is P.E.?
_____ students said their favorite school subject is P.E.

     (a) 5

     (b) 7

     (c) 10

4. Do more students like math or art?
More students like _____.

     (a) math

     (b) art

Create a Graph

What is your favorite subject?

My favorite subject is _____.

WORD BANK

Nouns (ideas)

math	social studies	_____
science	physical education	_____
English	art	_____

LANGUAGE TO **COMPARE**

I wrote that too.

I wrote the same answer.

Complete the table.

School Subject	Number of Students
math	
science	
English	
P.E. / physical education	
social studies	
art	

Create a Graph

Complete the graph with data from your class or group.

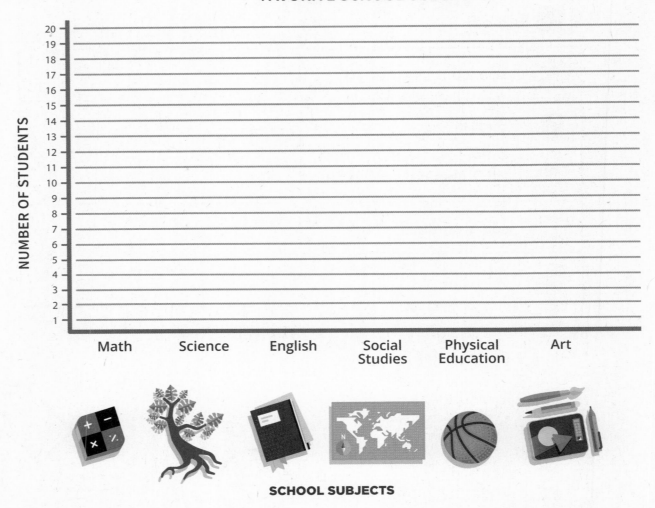

FAVORITE SCHOOL SUBJECTS

SCHOOL SUBJECTS

Write About It

Write sentences about your graph.

1. _____ students say their favorite subject is _____.
   (Number)   *(subject)*

2. My graph shows that _____ students chose _____.
                        (number)   *(subject)*

3. My graph also shows that _____ students chose _____.
                            (number)   *(subject)*

4. Students like _____!
   (subject)

LANGUAGE TO SHARE IDEAS 💬

What did you write?

I wrote _____.

Wonderful! Now you know all about school subjects.
Tell your partner about your favorite subject:
My favorite subject is (subject) because I like to (verb).

School Schedule

A schedule tells us when things happen at school. Let's learn how to talk about a school schedule.

 ## Vocabulary Builder

1. Say It   **2.** See It   **3.** Read It   **4.** Write It

week
week
(noun)

Every Sunday, we start a new **week**.

Word _____
      week
Translation _____

Make Connections _____

_____

day
day
(noun)

What **day** do we have soccer practice?

We have soccer practice on Thursday.

Word _____
      day
Translation _____

Make Connections _____

_____

time

time
(noun)

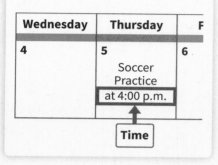

What **time** does soccer practice start?

It starts at 4:00 p.m.

Word _____
    time

Translation _____

Make Connections _____

_____

event

e • vent
(noun)

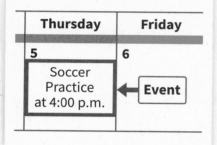

Soccer practice is an **event** I go to every week.

Word _____
    event

Translation _____

Make Connections _____

_____

morning

morn • ing
(noun)

We have social studies in the **morning**.

Word _____
    morning

Translation _____

Make Connections _____

_____

Vocabulary and Language

afternoon

af • ter • **noon**
(noun)

Daily Schedule: Thursday	
Time	**Event**
7:00–8:00	Before School: Breakfast
8:00–9:00	Social Studies
9:00–10:00	Math
10:00–11:00	Art
11:00–12:00	English
12:00–1:00	Lunch
1:00–2:00	Science
2:00–3:00	Physical Education
3:00–5:00	After School: Sports, Clubs, Tutoring

Noon = 12:00p.m.

Afternoon/p.m.

We have science after lunch in the **afternoon**.

Word _____
afternoon

Translation _____

Make Connections _____

_____

before

be • **fore**
(preposition)

Daily Schedule: Thursday	
Time	**Event**
7:00–8:00	Before School: Breakfast
8:00–9:00	Social Studies
9:00–10:00	Math
10:00–11:00	Art
11:00–12:00	English
12:00–1:00	Lunch
1:00–2:00	Science
2:00–3:00	Physical Education
3:00–5:00	After School: Sports, Clubs, Tutoring

Students eat breakfast in the cafeteria **before** school starts.

Word _____
before

Translation _____

Make Connections _____

_____

after

af • ter
(preposition)

Daily Schedule: Thursday	
Time	**Event**
7:00–8:00	Before School: Breakfast
8:00–9:00	Social Studies
9:00–10:00	Math
10:00–11:00	Art
11:00–12:00	English
12:00–1:00	Lunch
1:00–2:00	Science
2:00–3:00	Physical Education
3:00–5:00	After School: Sports, Clubs, Tutoring

Amir plays soccer **after** school.

Word _____
after

Translation _____

Make Connections _____

_____

Vocabulary Review

week	event	before
day	morning	after
time	afternoon	

Share translations with a partner.

> **LANGUAGE TO SHARE TRANSLATIONS** 💬
>
> Can you share a word in (language)?
> The (language) word for ____ is ____.

Write new sentences about your schedule.

1. I have _____ first in the **morning**.
   (noun)

2. _____ is an **event** I go to every week.
   (Noun)

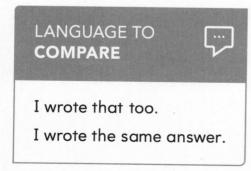

> **LANGUAGE TO COMPARE** 💬
>
> I wrote that too.
> I wrote the same answer.

Vocabulary and Language

 ## Language Builder

Schedule Words

Use **on**, **at**, **in**, **before**, or **after** to tell <u>when</u> something happens.

On a day of the week	*I have math class **<u>on</u> Monday**.*
At a specific time	*I have math class **<u>at</u> 9:30**.*
In the morning or the afternoon	*I have math class **<u>in</u> the morning**. I have music class **<u>in</u> the afternoon**.*
Before or **after** another event or class	*I have math class **<u>before</u> lunch**. I have soccer practice **<u>after</u> school**.*

Write the correct schedule word.

Model: Chen has computer class _____on_____ Friday.
(on/at)

1. Chen has breakfast _____ 8:00.
(on/at)

2. Chen has physical education _____ the morning.
(on/in)

3. Chen has art _____ the afternoon.
(on/in)

4. Chen has lunch _____ science class.
(before/in)

LANGUAGE TO
SHARE IDEAS

What did you choose?

I chose _____.

Listen Up

Listen to the conversation.

 Hello, Serene! When do you have science?

Hello, Mateo! I have science on Monday after lunch.

When do you have math?

I have math on Tuesday in the morning.

Talk About It

Partner A, ask questions. Partner B, respond. Then switch roles.

A: Hello, _____! When do you
    (Name)

have _____?
(class)

B: Hello! I have _____
        (class)

_____.
(on Day/every day)

A: When do you have _____?
        (class)

B: I have _____ in the
      (class)

_____.
(morning/afternoon)

WORD BANK

Classes		Days of the Week	
art	physical education	Monday	Friday
English	science	Tuesday	Saturday
math	social studies	Wednesday	Sunday
_____		Thursday	every day

Listen and Respond

Listen to the morning announcement from the principal.

Take notes on the announcement.

Topic: This Week's Activities

- Girls' basketball game on _____ after school

- Drama club performance on _____ after lunch

- Garden Club fruit sale _____ before and

  after school

- Science fair on _____ before lunch

WORD BANK

Days of the Week

Monday	Thursday	Sunday
Tuesday	Friday	every day
Wednesday	Saturday	

Answer the questions.

1. Which event is happening every day?

a

b

c

d

2. Which event is happening before lunch on Friday?

a

b

c

d

Write About It

 Remember!

Use **on**, **at**, **in**, **before**, and **after** to tell <u>when</u> something happens.

*I have art **<u>on</u>** <u>Friday</u>.*

*I have art **<u>at</u>** <u>1 p.m.</u>*

*I have art **<u>in</u>** <u>the afternoon</u>.*

*I have art **<u>before</u>** <u>math</u>.*

*I have art **<u>after</u>** <u>lunch</u>.*

WORD BANK

Nouns (things, ideas)

art	science
breakfast	social studies
drama club	sports
English	the afternoon
lunch	the morning
math	tutoring
physical education	

Write about Sonam's schedule for Thursday.

Daily Schedule: Thursday	
Time	Event
7:00–8:00	Before School: Breakfast
8:00–9:00	Social Studies
9:00–10:00	Math
10:00–11:00	Art
11:00–12:00	English
12:00–1:00	Lunch
1:00–2:00	Science
2:00–3:00	Physical Education
3:00–5:00	After School: Sports, Clubs, Tutoring

LANGUAGE TO COLLABORATE

What can we write?
We can write _____.

Sonam has a busy schedule on _____.
(Day of Week)

She has math _____ _____.
(before/after)   (noun)

She has English _____ _____.
(before/after)   (noun)

After lunch, she has _____ and
(noun)

_____. She has
(noun)

_____ _____ _____.
(noun)   (at/in/on)   (noun)

Write About It

Write about your school schedule for one day.

Model: I have a busy schedule on <u>Tuesday</u>. I have <u>science</u> <u>before</u> <u>math</u>. I have <u>art</u> <u>before</u> <u>lunch</u>. After lunch, I have <u>English</u> and <u>social studies</u>. I have <u>drama club</u> <u>in</u> <u>the afternoon</u>.

I have a busy schedule on _____.
　　　　　　　　　　　　　　　(Day of Week)

I have _____
　　　　(noun)

_____ _____.
(before/after)　　　　　　　　　　　　(noun)

I have _____
　　　　(noun)

_____ _____.
(before/after)　　　　　　　　　　　　(noun)

After lunch, I have _____
　　　　　　　　　　　　(noun)

and _____.
　　(noun)

I have _____
　　　　(noun)

_____ _____.
(at/in/on)　　　　　　　　　　　　　(noun)

WORD BANK

Nouns (things, ideas)

art

breakfast

drama club

English

lunch

math

physical education

science

social studies

sports

the afternoon

the morning

Days of the Week

Monday

Tuesday

Wednesday

Thursday

Friday

Amazing! Now you can talk about your school schedule. Tell your partner about your favorite class: *My favorite class is (noun). It is (before/after) (noun).*

In the Cafeteria

At school, students eat meals like breakfast and lunch in the cafeteria. Let's learn the steps for getting lunch in the cafeteria.

 ## Vocabulary Builder

1. Say It   **2.** See It   **3.** Read It   **4.** Write It

eat

eat
(verb)

Students **eat** in the cafeteria.

Word _____
    eat

Translation _____

Make Connections _____

_____

breakfast

break • fast
(noun)

Students eat **breakfast** in the morning.

Word _____
    breakfast

Translation _____

Make Connections _____

_____

lunch

lunch
(noun)

Students eat **lunch** around noon.

Word _____
        lunch

Translation _____

Make Connections _____

_____

wait

wait
(verb)

Students **wait** in line to get food.

Word _____
        wait

Translation _____

Make Connections _____

_____

take

take
(verb)

Students **take** a tray and a napkin.

Word _____
        take

Translation _____

Make Connections _____

_____

choose

choose
(verb)

Students **choose** what to eat for lunch.

Word _____
       choose

Translation _____

Make Connections _____

_____

sit

sit
(verb)

Students **sit** at a table with friends.

Word _____
      sit

Translation _____

Make Connections _____

_____

clean up

clean up
(verb)

Students **clean up** the table and go back to class.

Word _____
      clean up

Translation _____

Make Connections _____

_____

Vocabulary Review

eat

breakfast

lunch

wait

take

choose

sit

clean up

Share translations with a partner.

> LANGUAGE TO
> **SHARE TRANSLATIONS**
>
> Can you share a word in (language)?
> The (language) word for _____ is _____.

What are other words to use in the cafeteria?

These are other words to use in the cafeteria:

- _____

- _____

- _____

- _____

- _____

Language Builder

Sequence Words

Sequence words tell the order of events. Use sequence words to tell the steps for **how to do something**.

First, → *Then,* → *Also,* → *Next,* → *Finally,*

Use a **comma** after a sequence word.

First, *wait in line to get food.*

**Read the steps for getting food at school.
<u>Underline</u> the sequence words.**

Model: <u>First</u>, get your lunch. <u>Then</u>, eat your food.

1. First, wait in line.

2. Then, take a tray. Also, take a napkin, fork, and knife.

3. Next, choose your food.

4. Sit down at a table. Then, eat your lunch.

5. Finally, clean up the table.

**LANGUAGE TO
SHARE IDEAS**

What did you underline?

I underlined the sequence word _____.

Listen Up

Listen to the conversation.

 Hi, Chris! How do I get food in the cafeteria?

Hi, Maria! First, wait in line. Then, take a tray. Also, take a fork and spoon.

That makes sense! What do I do next?

Next, choose your food and a drink. Then, find an empty seat. Finally, sit down at a table.

Talk About It

Partner A, **ask questions.** Partner B, **respond. Then switch roles.**

A: Hi, _____! How do I get food
(Name)
in the cafeteria?

B: Hello, _____. First, _____ in line.
(Name)   (verb)
Then, take a _____. Also, _____
(noun)   (verb)
a fork and spoon.

A: That makes sense! What do I do next?

B: Next, _____
(verb)
your _____ and a drink.
(noun)
Then, find an empty _____.
(noun)
Finally, _____ down at a table.
(verb)

Make Observations

Look at the pictures. Discuss what you see. Take notes to help you.

1. _____
   _____
   _____
   _____

2. _____
   _____
   _____
   _____

3. _____
   _____
   _____
   _____

4. _____
   _____
   _____
   _____

5. _____
_____
_____
_____

6. _____
_____
_____
_____

WORD BANK 🧩

Nouns (things)

| drink | fork and spoon | napkin | table |
| food | line | seat | tray |

LANGUAGE TO **OBSERVE** 💬

What do you see?

I see _____.

What else do you see?

I also see _____.

Read and Respond

Read the text. Then answer the questions.

Students **eat breakfast** and **lunch** in the cafeteria. Do you know what to do? First, **wait** in line. Then, **take** a tray. Also, take a napkin, fork, and knife. Next, **choose** your food. Do you want an apple or a banana? Don't forget a drink! Then, **sit** down at a table and eat. Finally, **clean up** and go back to class.

1. According to the text, what should students do first?

a

b

c

d

2. According to the text, what should students do second?

a

b

c

d

3. According to the text, what should students do after they eat?

a

b

c

d

Write About It

 Don't Forget!

Use **sequence words** to tell how to do something. Put a **comma** after the sequence word, then write the step.

First, *wait in line.* ***Then,*** *get your food.*

Complete the steps to explain how to get food in the cafeteria.

LANGUAGE TO COLLABORATE

What can we write?

We can write _____.

1. Wait in _____ .
   (noun)

2. Take a _____ and a _____ .
   (noun)   *(noun)*

3. Find an empty _____ and
   (noun)

   _____ down at a table.
   (verb)

4. _____ your food.
   (Verb)

5. Clean up the _____ .
   (noun)

WORD BANK

Nouns (things)		Verbs (action words)	
drink	napkin	choose	get
food	seat	clean up	sit
fork and spoon	table	eat	take
line	tray	find	wait

Use sequence words to write the steps for getting food.

It is easy to get your lunch in the cafeteria. _____

_____

_____

_____

_____

_____

WORD BANK	

Sequence Words

First,　　　Also,　　　Next,　　　Then,　　　Finally,

Woo-hoo! You just learned about the cafeteria. Now, tell your partner what you do first in the cafeteria: *First, I (verb phrase).*

Getting Around School

How do you get to the main office? I can tell you! Let's learn how to give directions at school.

Vocabulary Builder

1. Say It   **2.** See It   **3.** Read It   **4.** Write It

left

left
(adverb)

Turn **left** to get to the computers.

Word _____
       left

Translation _____

Make Connections _____

_____

right

right
(adverb)

Turn **right**. You will see the book shelves.

Word _____
       right

Translation _____

Make Connections _____

_____

straight

straight
(adverb)

Go **straight** to get to the librarian's desk.

Word _____
    straight

Translation _____

Make Connections _____

_____

downstairs

down • stairs
(adverb)

Go **downstairs** to get to the cafeteria.

Word _____
    downstairs

Translation _____

Make Connections _____

_____

upstairs

up • stairs
(adverb)

Go **upstairs** to get to the library.

Word _____
    upstairs

Translation _____

Make Connections _____

_____

Vocabulary and Language

inside

in • side
(adverb)

I am **inside** my school.

Word _____
    inside

Translation _____

Make Connections _____

_____

outside

out • side
(adverb)

I am **outside** in front of the school.

Word _____
    outside

Translation _____

Make Connections _____

_____

through

through
(preposition)

Go **through** that door.

Word _____
    through

Translation _____

Make Connections _____

_____

Vocabulary Review

left	downstairs	outside
right	upstairs	through
straight	inside	

Share translations with a partner.

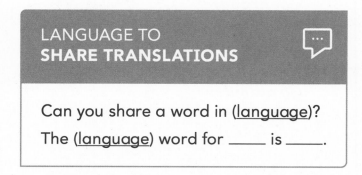

LANGUAGE TO
SHARE TRANSLATIONS

Can you share a word in (language)?

The (language) word for ____ is ____.

Write new sentences about your school.

1. Go **inside** to get to the _____.
   (noun)

2. Go **outside** and walk across the _____.
   (noun)

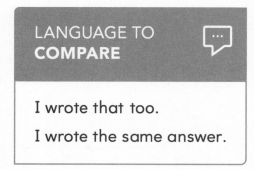

LANGUAGE TO
COMPARE

I wrote that too.

I wrote the same answer.

Language Builder

Direction Words

A **direction word** tells you where to go. Use <u>go</u> or <u>turn</u> before **direction words** when giving directions.

<u>Go</u> **straight**.	<u>Go</u> **through**.
<u>Go</u> **upstairs**.	<u>Go</u> **downstairs**.
<u>Go</u> **inside**.	<u>Go</u> **outside**.
<u>Turn</u> **right**.	<u>Turn</u> **left**.

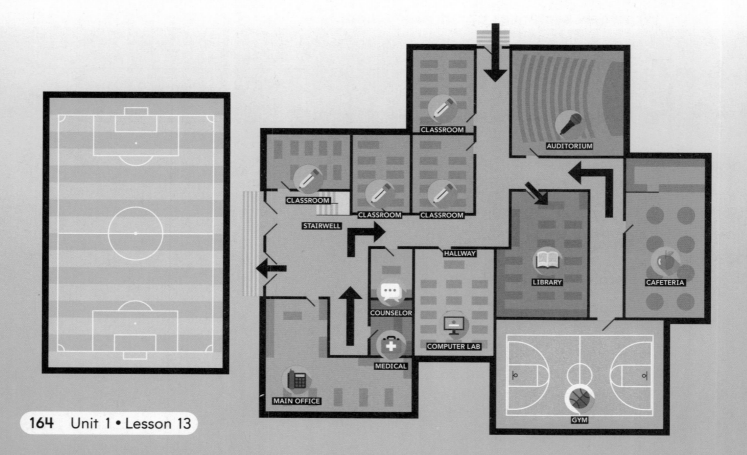

Write the directions that go with each image.

_____

_____

_____

_____

Listen Up

Listen to the conversation.

▶ Hi, Shaun! How do I get to the library?

Hi, Taikhira! First, go upstairs. Then, turn right.

OK. So first I go upstairs, and then I turn right?

Yes! That is how you get to the library.

Talk About It

Partner A, **ask questions.** Partner B, **respond. Then switch roles.**

A: Hi, _____!
   (Name)

   How do I get to the _____?
                       (noun)

B: Hi, _____!
   (Name)

   First, _____. Then, _____.
          (directions)   (directions)

A: Thanks! So first I _____, and
                      (directions)

   then I _____?
          (directions)

B: Yes! That is how you get to the _____.
                                   (noun)

WORD BANK

Nouns (places)		Directions	
bathroom	hallway	turn left	go straight
cafeteria	library	turn right	go through
classroom	main office	go upstairs	go inside
gym	schoolyard	go downstairs	go outside

Reading a Map

A school **map** shows where places are in the school building.

To read a map:

1. Find your location, or place, on the map.

2. Find the destination, or place you want to go.

3. Move your finger from your location to the place you want to go. Follow hallways and stairs.

Read and Respond

Read the map to find the gym and the main office.

Write the correct direction words to tell how to go from the gym to the main office.

1. From the gym, go _____ the door.
   (through/right)

2. Go _____ .
   (right/straight)

3. Turn _____ .
   (left/right)

4. Go past the _____ .
   (cafeteria/library)

5. At the end of the hallway, turn _____ .
   (left/right)

6. Turn _____ .
   (left/right)

7. After the counselor's office, turn _____ .
   (left/right)

LANGUAGE TO SHARE IDEAS

What did you write?

I wrote _____ .

Create a Map

Work with your teacher and classmates to draw a map
of your school or a part of your school.

 ## Write About It

 Remember!

Use <u>go</u> or <u>turn</u> before **direction words** when giving directions.

<u>Go</u> **inside**. *<u>Turn</u>* **right**.

WORD BANK

Nouns (places)			Directions		
bathroom	gym	main office	turn left	go downstairs	go outside
cafeteria	hallway	schoolyard	turn right	go straight	go inside
classroom	library		go upstairs	go through	

Write sentences to give directions to places at your school.

Model: How do I get to the _____?

      To get to the _____, first, _____. Then, _____.
                 (place at school)   *(directions)*   *(directions)*

1. How do I get to the _____?
      (place at school)

    To get to the _____,
      (place at school)

    first, _____.
      (directions)

    Then, _____.
      (directions)

2. How do I get to the _____?
      (place at school)

    To get to the _____,
      (place at school)

    first, _____.
      (directions)

    Then, _____.
      (directions)

LANGUAGE TO COLLABORATE

What can we write?

We can write _____.

Well done! You just learned how to give directions. Now, tell your partner how you will get to your next class: *First, I will go (direction word). Then, I will go (direction word).*

Explain "How to" at School

Now that you have learned about people, places, and actions at school, you can teach new students how to do something at your school!

View a Student Model

Read this poster created by a student.

How to Meet New Friends
by Alana R.

It's easy to meet new friends!

Step 1. Walk up to the person you want to meet.

Step 2. Say hello, hi, or ¡Hola!

Step 3. Introduce yourself and tell them your name.

Step 4. Ask what their name is.

Step 5. Share information about yourself.

¡Hola! My name is Alana. What's your name?

Label the parts of the poster.

author	image	steps	title

Project Prompt

Create a presentation to explain to new students how to do something academic or social at school. Use sequence words to tell the steps in order.

 ## Mark Elements

Read the student model. Mark the elements.

How to Meet New Friends
by Alana R.

It's easy to meet new friends. First, walk up to the person you want to meet. Then, introduce yourself and tell them your name. Next, ask what their name is. Then, share information about yourself. Finally, say "hello" or "hi" when you see them at school.

1. <u>Underline</u> the sequence words, such as *First* and *Then*.

2. Highlight in yellow the verbs, or action words.

3. Highlight in blue the nouns, or people, places, things, and ideas.

Project Prompt

Create a presentation to explain to new students how to do something academic or social at school. Use sequence words to tell the steps in order.

Brainstorm Ideas

What do you know how to do at school?

Academic (school/learning)	Social (friends)
• check out a library book	• join an after-school club
• _____	• _____
_____	_____
• _____	• _____
_____	_____

LANGUAGE TO SHARE IDEAS

What did you write?

I wrote _____.

Review Vocabulary

Identify words or phrases from the unit to use in your writing.

Nouns	Verbs
_____	_____
_____	_____
_____	_____

Write Together

Write about how to do something <u>academic</u> at school.

1. Write the title and a topic sentence.

Title: How to Check Out a Library Book

Topic Sentence: It's easy to _____.
  (verb phrase)

2. Draft the steps.

Step 1: Go to the _____.
  (noun for place)

Step 2: Find the book you want to _____.
  (verb phrase)

Step 3: Take the book to the _____.
  (noun for place)

Step 4: Ask the _____ if you can check out the book.
  (noun for person)

Step 5: Take the _____ home to read.
  (noun for thing)

Write Together

3. Draft the paragraph.

It's easy to _____. First, go to
   (verb phrase)

the _____. Then, find the book
   (noun for place)

you want to _____. Next, take the book
   (verb phrase)

to the _____. Then, ask
   (noun for place)

the _____ if you can check out the book.
   (noun for person)

Finally, take the _____ home to read.
   (noun for thing)

Write With a Partner

Write about how to do something <u>social</u> at school.

1. Write the title and topic sentence.

Title: How to Join an After-School Club

Topic Sentence: It's easy to _____
   (verb phrase)

_____.

2. Draft the steps.

Step 1: _____ about school clubs in the _____.
(verb: Read, Learn, Ask)   (noun for place)

Step 2: Choose the _____ you want to join.
                  (noun)

Step 3: Learn the time and _____ of the club's meetings.
                               (noun)

Step 4: Ask _____ if you can sign up.
            (noun for person)

Step 5: Go to the _____.
                 (noun)

> **LANGUAGE TO COLLABORATE** 💬
>
> What can we write?
> We can write _____.

3. Draft the paragraph.

It's easy to _____. First, _____
           (verb phrase)   (verb: read, learn, ask)

about school clubs in the _____. Then, choose
                            (noun for place)

the _____ you want to join. Next, learn the time and
    (noun)

_____ of the club's meetings. Then, ask _____
(noun)   (noun for person)

if you can sign up. Finally, go to the _____.
                                  (noun)

Project Prompt

Create a presentation to explain to new students how to do something academic or social at school. Use sequence words to tell the steps in order.

 ## Choose a Prompt

Select a task for your project:

☐ how to do something academic at school

☐ how to do something social at school

 ## Write the Topic

Write the title and topic sentence for your draft.

Title: How to _____
　　　　　　　(Topic)

Topic sentence: It's easy to _____
　　　　　　　　　　　　　(verb phrase)

_____ .

LANGUAGE TO SHARE IDEAS 💬

What did you write?

I wrote _____ .

Write the Steps

Write the steps for your "how to" in order. Start each step with a verb.

Step 1: _____

_____

Step 2: _____

_____

Step 3. _____

_____

Step 4: _____

_____

Step 5: _____

_____

Write a Paragraph

Write the steps using complete sentences.

_____
(Title)

by _____
   (Name)

It's easy to _____
       (verb phrase)

_____.

_____, _____
(Sequence word)   (step 1)

_____.

_____, _____
(Sequence word)   (step 2)

_____.

_____, _____
(Sequence word)   (step 3)

_____.

_____, _____
(Sequence word)   (step 4)

_____.

_____, _____
(Sequence word)   (step 5)

_____.

Check and Edit

Use this checklist to review and edit your draft.

Did you . . .

☐ write five steps in the correct order?

☐ use a verb in each step?

☐ use an uppercase letter for the first letter of a name?

☐ spell vocabulary words correctly?

 ## Create a Poster

Choose your final project format. Then create your poster.

▢ Print Poster	▢ Digital Poster
1. Write your ideas on paper. 2. Add images by drawing or cutting and pasting pictures.	1. Type your ideas on the computer. 2. Add images by searching online or taking pictures and uploading them.
Optional: Make it multilingual by adding translations.	

Speak at the Right Volume

When you share ideas during class, **speak at the right volume** for your audience.

- With a **partner**, speak loudly enough so that your partner can hear you, but not so loudly that you distract others.

- When presenting to the **class**, speak loudly enough so that everyone can hear you.

Partner Practice

Share your poster with a partner. Speak at the right volume. Then switch roles.

LANGUAGE TO **GIVE FEEDBACK** 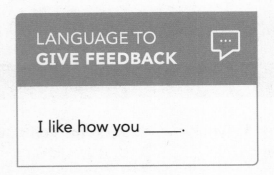
I like how you _____.

WORD BANK

Feedback
spoke loudly
knew the information
used a helpful image

Present Posters

Share your poster with the group or class.
Speak at the right volume when you present.

Listen and Take Notes

Listen to your classmates and take notes on their topics.

Classmate's Name	"How-To" Topic
• _____	• _____
• _____	• _____
• _____	• _____

 ## Reflect

Write one way you can improve your next presentation.

One way I can improve my next presentation is to _____

_____.

WORD BANK

**Verb Phrases
(action phrases)**

speak louder

practice more

You did it! You finished Unit 1 and learned all about school. Congratulations!

Language Expectations and Goals

Unit 1: Welcome to School

Before each lesson, preview the lesson goals. When you complete
a lesson, mark the box ☑ next to each goal you reached.

Lesson 1	Welcome to School

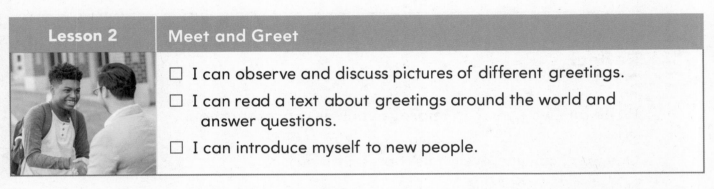

- ☐ I can watch a video to learn about school.
- ☐ I can take notes on a video using new words.
- ☐ I can ask and answer questions about school.

Lesson 2	Meet and Greet

- ☐ I can observe and discuss pictures of different greetings.
- ☐ I can read a text about greetings around the world and
answer questions.
- ☐ I can introduce myself to new people.

Lesson 3	From A to Z

The English Alphabet

Aa	Bb	Cc	Dd	Ee	Ff
Gg	Hh	Ii	Jj	Kk	Ll
Mm	Nn	Oo	Pp	Qq	Rr
Ss	Tt	Uu	Vv	Ww	Xx
Yy	Zz				

- ☐ I can read and write the letters of the alphabet.
- ☐ I can write and spell my name.
- ☐ I can put names in alphabetical order.
- ☐ I can write sentences using uppercase letters for names of people.

Lesson 4 — From 0 to 100

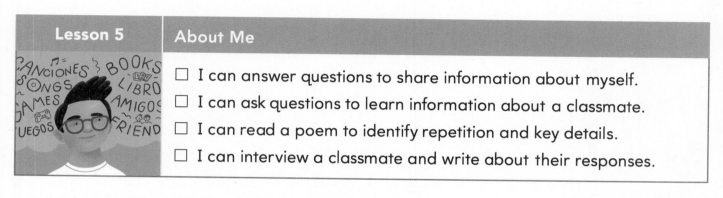

- ☐ I can count to 100.
- ☐ I can write numbers 0 to 100.
- ☐ I can say and write sentences with numbers.
- ☐ I can observe a picture and talk about it using numbers.

Lesson 5 — About Me

- ☐ I can answer questions to share information about myself.
- ☐ I can ask questions to learn information about a classmate.
- ☐ I can read a poem to identify repetition and key details.
- ☐ I can interview a classmate and write about their responses.

Lesson 6 — People at School

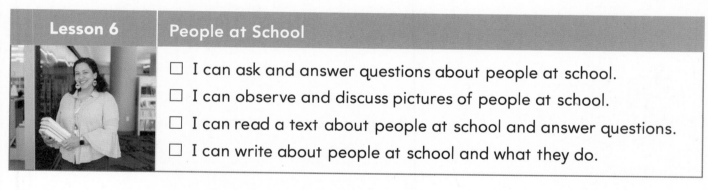

- ☐ I can ask and answer questions about people at school.
- ☐ I can observe and discuss pictures of people at school.
- ☐ I can read a text about people at school and answer questions.
- ☐ I can write about people at school and what they do.

Lesson 7 — School Supplies

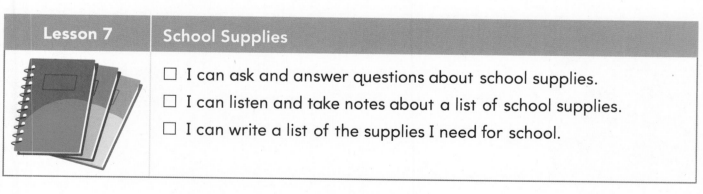

- ☐ I can ask and answer questions about school supplies.
- ☐ I can listen and take notes about a list of school supplies.
- ☐ I can write a list of the supplies I need for school.

Goals and Achievements

Lesson 8	Class Acts

☐ I can ask and answer questions about what we do at school.

☐ I can read a speech and write about the main ideas.

☐ I can talk and write about what I do at school.

Lesson 9	Places at School

☐ I can ask and answer questions about places at school.

☐ I can observe and discuss a picture of places at school.

☐ I can read a text about places at school and answer questions.

☐ I can write about where things happen at school.

Lesson 10	School Subjects

☐ I can ask and answer questions about favorite school subjects.

☐ I can read a bar graph and answer questions.

☐ I can create a bar graph and write about it.

Lesson 11	School Schedule

☐ I can ask and answer questions about school schedules.

☐ I can listen to an announcement and take notes.

☐ I can write about my school schedule.

Lesson 12	**In the Cafeteria**

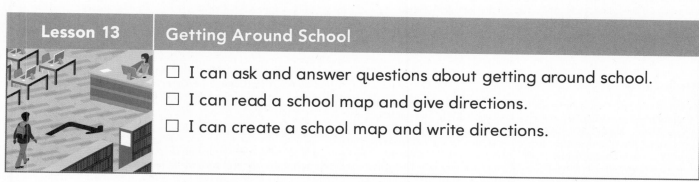

- ☐ I can ask and answer questions about getting food in the cafeteria.
- ☐ I can observe and discuss images showing how to get food in the cafeteria.
- ☐ I can read a text about getting food in the cafeteria and answer questions.
- ☐ I can write the steps for getting food in the cafeteria.

Lesson 13	**Getting Around School**

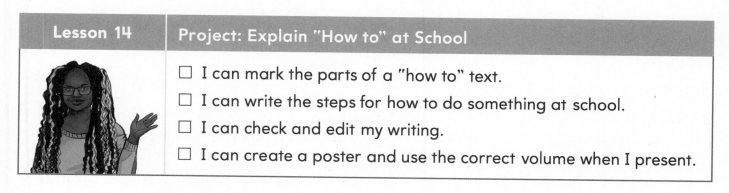

- ☐ I can ask and answer questions about getting around school.
- ☐ I can read a school map and give directions.
- ☐ I can create a school map and write directions.

Lesson 14	**Project: Explain "How to" at School**

- ☐ I can mark the parts of a "how to" text.
- ☐ I can write the steps for how to do something at school.
- ☐ I can check and edit my writing.
- ☐ I can create a poster and use the correct volume when I present.

Unit Reflections

My favorite lesson in this unit was _____

_____.

In **Unit 2**, I want to improve my skills in:

- ☐ speaking
- ☐ reading
- ☐ listening
- ☐ writing

Credits

About Me: "Bilingual"/ "Bilingüe" by Alma Flor Ada, from *The Poetry Friday Anthology for Celebrations*, edited by Sylvia Vardell and Janet Wong. Copyright © 2015 by Alma Flor Ada. Used by permission of the author.

Class Acts: Obama, B. (2009, September 8). Remarks by the President in a National Address to America's Schoolchildren. Wakefield High School, Arlington, VA

Anchor Video

science lab ©Michael Chamberlin/Shutterstock, *auditorium* ©lichaoshu/Adobe Stock, *gymnasium* ©John Giustina/The Image Bank/Getty Images

Welcome to School

school ©littleny/Adobe Stock; *teacher* ©Monkey Business Images/Shutterstock; *raising hand* ©Drazen Zigic/Shutterstock; *students in hall* ©Monkey Business Images/Shutterstock; *reading book* ©Hill Street Studios/Digital Vision/Getty Images; *taking test* ©Chris Ryan/Caia Image/Media Bakery; *student listening* ©kali9/iStock/Getty Images; *students talking* ©SDI Productions/E+/Getty Images

Meet and Greet

waving hello ©Art_Photo/Shutterstock; *students in hallway* ©FangXiaNuo/E+/Getty Images; *waving hello on laptop* ©Mayur Kakade/Moment/Getty Images; *shaking hands* ©SDI Productions/E+/Getty Images; *students in class* ©Stígur Már Karlsson/Heimsmyndir/E+/Getty Images; *hand over heart* ©Wayhome Studio/Adobe Stock; *waving goodbye* ©Makistock/Shutterstock; *waving hello* ©Art_Photo/Shutterstock; *day cycle* ©Maria_Galybina/Shutterstock; *shaking hands* ©Maskot/Media Bakery; *traditional Japanese greeting* ©stockstudioX/E+/Getty Images; *air kiss* ©AntonioDiaz/Shutterstock; *Maori greeting* ©nazar_ab/E+/Getty Images; *grandfather and grandchildren* ©Kong Ding Chek/E+/Getty Images

From 0 to 100

football players ©Cavan Images/Getty Images

About Me

geography class ©Myrleen Pearson/Alamy; *students on campus* ©Kentaroo Tryman/Maskot Images/Media Bakery; *student in front of chalkboard* ©StunningArt/Shutterstock; *students working* ©Maskot/Media Bakery; *birthday* ©Carol Yepes/Moment/Getty Images

People at School

principal ©kali9/Getty Images; *talking on phone* ©Goodluz/Shutterstock; *basketball coach* ©miodrag ignjatovic/E+/Getty Images; *counselor* ©Monkey Business Images/Shutterstock; *custodian* ©LifestyleVisuals/E+/Getty Images; *school cafeteria* ©Yellow Dog Productions/The Image Bank/Getty Images; *librarian* ©SDI Productions/E+/Getty Images; *nurse and patient* ©Rob/Adobe Stock

School Supplies

blue school backpack ©Mike Flippo/Shutterstock; *textbook* ©Sam Dudgeon/HMH; *calculator* ©HMH; *laptop* ©Sergio Sergo/Shutterstock; *folder* ©HMH; *notebook* ©Mega Pixel/Shutterstock; *pen* ©PaoloGaetano/iStockPhoto; *pencil* ©Ahmet Misirligul/Shutterstock; *teacher* ©Monkey Business Images/Shutterstock

Class Acts

talking to teacher ©Rido/Dreamstime; *students hanging out* ©Monkey Business Images/Shutterstock; *science class* ©SDI Productions/E+/Getty Images; *volleyball team* ©South_agency/E+/Getty Images; *playing basketball* ©Marcos/Adobe Stock; *writing on white board* ©Rido/Shutterstock; *student studying* ©Jasmin Merdan/Moment/Getty Images; *raising hand* ©SDI Productions/E+/Getty Images; *Obama speaking* ©Kevin Dietsch/UPI/Alamy

Places at School

washing hands ©chpua/E+/Getty Images; *eating in cafeteria* ©Monkey Business Images/Dreamstime; *classroom* ©Monkey Business Images/Shutterstock; *basketball players* ©Hill Street Studios/Digital Vision/Getty Images; *students in school* ©Monkey Business Images/Shutterstock; *student studying* ©FatCamera/E+/Getty Images; *school secretary* ©Jim West/Alamy; *group of students* ©Monkey Business Images/Shutterstock

School Subjects

education symbols ©hilch/Adobe Stock; *students talking* ©SDI Productions/E+/Getty Images; *girl at board* ©Rido/Shutterstock; *science class* ©SolStock/Getty Images; *students at world map* ©Maskot/Getty Images; *students painting* ©Hill Street Studios/Digital Vision/Getty Images; *sports team* ©Rawpixel.com/Adobe Stock; *student with microscope* ©FatCamera/E+/Getty Images

In the Cafeteria

breakfast ©Jupiterimages/Getty Images; *school lunch* ©HMH

Project

students in hallway ©FangXiaNuo/E+/Getty Images

Language Expecations and Goals

shaking hands ©SDI Productions/E+/Getty Images; *librarian* ©SDI Productions/E+/Getty Images; *football players* ©Cavan Images/Getty Images; *raising hand* ©SDI Productions/E+/Getty Images; *students in school* ©Monkey Business Images/Shutterstock

Speaking and Listening characters

Serene illustration adapted from ©Johner Images/Alamy; *Mateo illustration adapted from* ©HMH; *Shaun illustration adapted from* ©nuiiko/Adobe Stock; *Taikhira illustration adapted from* ©Silverblack/Dreamstime; *Chris illustration adapted from* ©Ajphotos/Dreamstime; *Maria illustration adapted from* ©digitalskillet/Getty Images